Understanding The Alphabet of the Dead Sea Scrolls

Development • Chronology • Dating

ADA YARDENI

cartaJerusalem

CONTENTS

First published in 2014 by
CARTA Jerusalem

Copyright © 2014
Carta Jerusalem, Ltd.
18 Ha'uman Street, P.O.B. 2500,
Jerusalem 9102401, Israel
E-mail: carta@carta.co.il
www.carta-jerusalem.com

Editor: Barbara L. Ball
Drawings © Ada Yardeni
Topography (page 4): Prof. Pinchas Yoeli

ISBN: 978-965-220-858-3

Printed in Israel

DEFINITIONS

Ancient Hebrew script—see "Palaeo-Hebrew".

Aramaic language and script—the official Semitic language and script used in the Persian Empire, mainly in the 5th–4th centuries BCE. The script, which consists of 21 graphic signs, gave birth to the Hebrew "square" script used from the 3rd century BCE to the present day.

"Arm"—the right stroke of Alef and Tsadi and the middle and right strokes of Shin.

Base-stroke—the lower, horizontal stroke of a letter (as opposed to the "roof").

Book-hand—the script style used by professional scribes for writing official texts.

Bullae—seal impressions on clay used for sealing and showing ownership.

Calligraphy—the art of "beautiful" writing.

Clay tablet—used mainly for the inscribing of cuneiform texts.

Copyist—a professional scribe who copied manuscripts.

Cursive script—an independent variant of a script style, resulting mainly from rapid writing.

Down-stroke—the stroke drawn vertically or slanting downwards.

Early or Ancient Hebrew script—see "Palaeo-Hebrew".

Elephantine—an island on the Nile River in Egypt, where many documents in the official Aramaic language and script were discovered, mainly dating from the Persian period.

Epigraphy—the study of ancient texts.

Flourishes—additions to the basic strokes of the letter-forms, which often became integral parts of the strokes.

Graphic evolution of the letter-forms—changes in the graphic forms of letters in a certain script style over time.

"Hook"—a short stroke slanting down to the left from the top of a vertical stroke, mainly in Waw, Yod and Lamed and occasionally in other letters.

Horizontal stroke—the stroke drawn horizontally or slanting from left to right or from right to left.

Imaginary baseline—an unmarked base line of the letters sharing an average height.

"Jewish" script—the script used in Judaea from the late 3rd century BCE until about 140 CE.

"Leg"—a vertical stroke in letters which have no base-stroke.

Letter signs—the graphic forms of a letter.

lingua franca—the international language used for communication.

Loop-fashion—a style of writing, mainly in the 1st century, in which certain strokes of the letters begin or end with a curve in the form of a loop.

"Mast" of Lamed—the upper, long stroke of the letter Lamed.

Mixed script—a script consisting of various letter forms of different script styles.

"Nabataean" script—one of the offshoots of the official Aramaic script, used by the population in the region later called by the Romans "the province of Arabia." From this script the modern Arabic script evolved in about the 3rd century CE. The earliest inscription in Nabataean script is from the 1st century BCE.

Nib—the top of the pen prepared for writing.

Ostraca—shards of broken clay vessels used as a surface for writing, mainly in ink.

Palaeo-Hebrew—the ancient Hebrew script, serving for the writing of ancient Hebrew texts from about the mid-9th century BCE; also called "Da'ats" or "Ra'ats" in Talmudic literature.

Palaeography—the study of ancient writing.

Papyrus—a plant used for producing sheets that served as a surface for writing, until about the 8th century CE (also used for other purposes).

Pictograms—images depicting words, syllables or letters.

Pre-"Jewish" script—the script of Jewish manuscripts of the late 3rd and early 2nd centuries BCE.

Reed pen—an implement made from reeds for writing in paint or ink on papyrus or on clay shards.

"Roof"—the upper horizontal stroke.

Scribal exercise—exercises for attaining skills in writing, usually consisting of parts of letters.

Scribe—in ancient times, a person trained in writing and copying texts of various kinds.

Script style—a certain script system commonly used by people in a certain place and at a certain time.

Semi-cursive script—a script with characteristics of both a book-hand and a cursive hand.

"Serif"—the protrusion at the top of the "roof" of a letter, created by the writing implement when it touches the writing surface at the beginning of the execution of the letter-form.

"Skeleton" of the letter—the basic structure of the individual letter sign.

Strokes—the individual lines of each letter-sign.

Stylus—a writing implement made of hard material used for inscribing on clay tablets or on wax.

"Tail" (of Bet)—the part of the base-stroke of Bet which continues to the right beyond the meeting point of the base-stroke and the down-stroke.

Tetragrammaton—the four Hebrew letters (Yod, He, Waw, He—YHWH) for the Divine name.

Vulgar script—writing by an untrained hand.

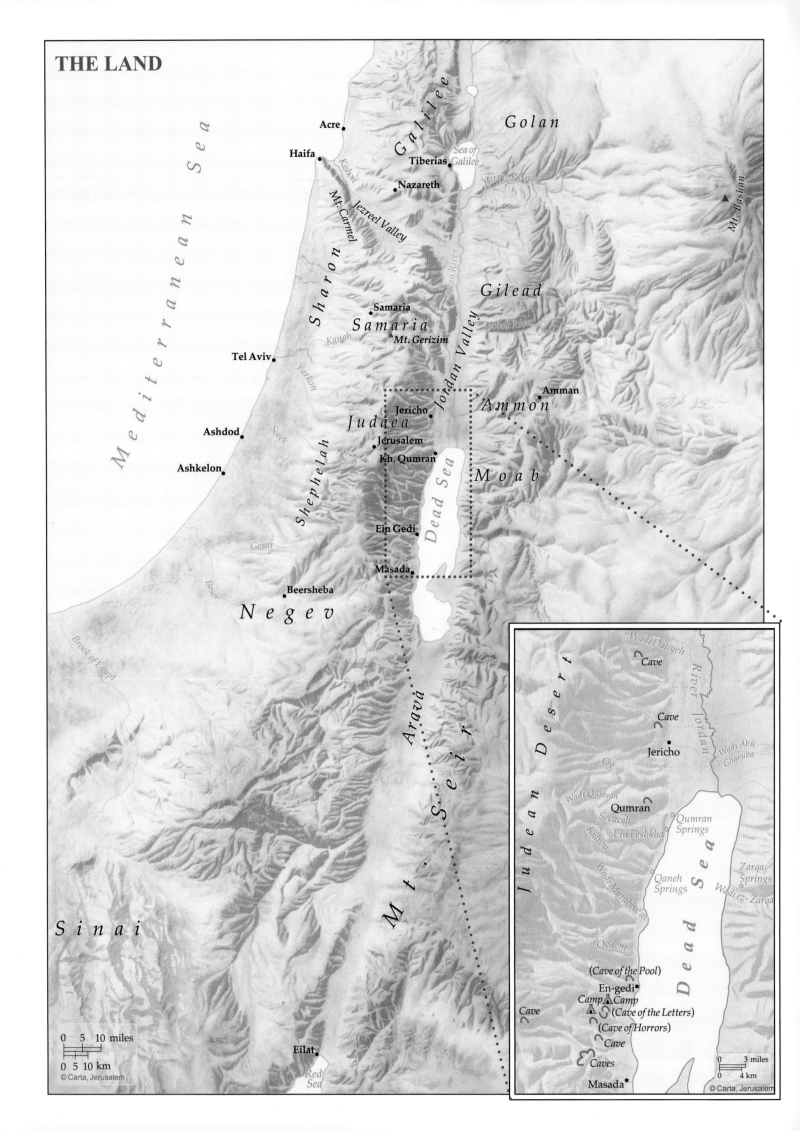

THE LAND

Mediterranean Sea

Galilee

Golan

Acre

Haifa

Sea of Galilee

Tiberias

Nazareth

Kishon

Mt. Carmel

Jezreel Valley

Yarmuk River

Mt. Bashan

Sharon

Jordan River

Gilead

Samaria

Samaria

Kanah

Mt. Gerizim

Jabbok River

Tel Aviv

Yarkon

Jordan Valley

Amman

Ammon

Jericho

Judaea

Ashdod

Sorek

Jerusalem

Kh. Qumran

Moab

Ashkelon

Shephelah

Dead Sea

Gerar

Ein Gedi

Besor

Masada

Beersheba

N e g e v

Arava

Mt. Seir

Brook of Egypt

S i n a i

0	5	10 miles
0	5 10 km	

© Carta, Jerusalem

Eilat

Red Sea

Inset

Wadi Daliyeh

River Jordan

Cave

Judean Desert

Cave

Wadi Abu Gharuba

Jericho

Og

Wadi Qumran

Qumran

Qumran Springs

Secacah

Ein Feshkha

Kidron

Qaneh Springs

Wadi Murabba'at

Dead Sea

Zarqa Springs

Qedem

Wadi ez-Zarqa

(Cave of the Pool)

En-gedi

Camp ▲ Camp
▲

(Cave of the Letters)

(Cave of Horrors)

Cave

Cave

Caves

Masada

0	3 miles
0	4 km

© Carta, Jerusalem

FOREWORD

This impressive book by Dr. Ada Yardeni makes it easy to understand why one never hears a single criticism of Ada Yardeni's professional abilities as a paleographer. It could be entitled "All you ever need to know about Hebrew paleography." Dr. Ada Yardeni stands at the head of her field, and this book is the best ever produced on the topic, though it owes much to those who have gone before, such as Frank Moore Cross, Jr., Nahman Avigad and Joseph Naveh.

The book excels in so many ways: its comprehensive survey of current Hebrew and Aramaic paleographic research, its aesthetically pleasing layout, its prolific examples, its attention to detail, and simplicity of style, all of which will appeal to professional and lay readers alike.

Beginning with concise definitions of terms in the field, Dr. Yardeni offers a careful description of how letters were formed on various materials, and in various times and locations over many centuries. With didactically sophisticated but simple explanations of what is a rather complicated field, the book masterfully describes the information it is possible to glean from a careful, even minute, examination of the letters and words of ancient Hebrew and Aramaic documents. It is a book written by a seasoned teacher, who knows how to lead the reader from the very first steps in the field into all the knowledge that must be assimilated by anyone who aspires to begin the long journey toward at least a partial expertise in the analysis of ancient Hebrew and Aramaic inscriptions and texts.

As a summary at the end of the book Dr. Yardeni concludes with a convenient list of indicators of the various stages of development of the scripts of the Judaean Desert documents. By demonstrating how these indicators are used in dating she initiates the reader into the many details of paleography which Dr. Yardeni herself takes into account when she is describing and dating a script or a document. One has the feeling she has provided a glimpse of the very inner workings of her mind; indeed, that she has divulged to the reader her "trade secrets."

This book sets a new standard in the field of ancient Hebrew and Aramaic paleography.

Weston W. Fields, Ph.D.
Executive Director
THE DEAD SEA SCROLLS FOUNDATION
November 2014

Introduction

The earliest biblical text discovered to date is part of the priestly benediction (Num 6:24–26) incised in early Hebrew letters (fig. 1) on two tiny silver plaques found in a burial cave in Jerusalem. Their script may be dated to about the early sixth century BCE (fig. 2). This early Hebrew script was used in the Land of Israel from the time its letter-signs began to show a significant deviation from those of the Phoenician letter-signs, in about the mid-ninth century BCE (fig. 3). The Phoenician writing system was adopted by neighboring countries for various languages, such as Hebrew, Aramaic, and Greek. This script system is called Alphabet after the early names of its two first letter-signs (meaning "bull" and "house," respectively, the ancient pictograms from which the linear forms gradually evolved, becoming a system of 22 letter-signs [figs. 4a, b]). "Alphabet" is the designation used to this day for all its offshoots.

Political events influenced the history of the script ever since its inception. The changes occurring in the early Hebrew script mainly reflect a *mutual influence of the forms of the letters created by the rapid writing in ink or paint and*

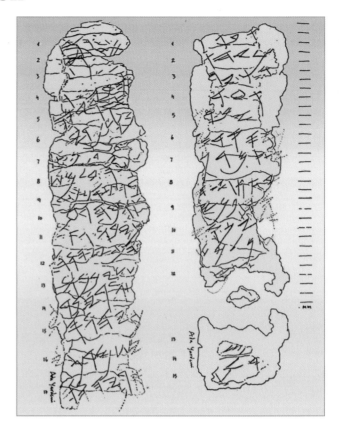

Fig. 1 (*above*). *Amulets with the Priestly Benediction written in Ancient Hebrew script.*

Fig. 2. *Comparative chart of the script of the Priestly Benediction amulets*

1. Hebrew seals, 7th cent. BCE;

2. Meṣad Ḥashavyahu letter, c. 625 BCE;

3. Arad Hebrew ostraca, early 6th cent. BCE;

4. Lachish letters, c. 597, 588 BCE;

5. Gibeon jar handles, 6th cent. BCE;

6. Ketef Hinnom seal;

7. Ketef Hinnom plaque 1;

8. Ketef Hinnom plaque 2;

9. Khirbet Beit Lei inscriptions, 6th cent. BCE

1	2	3	4	5	6	7	8	9

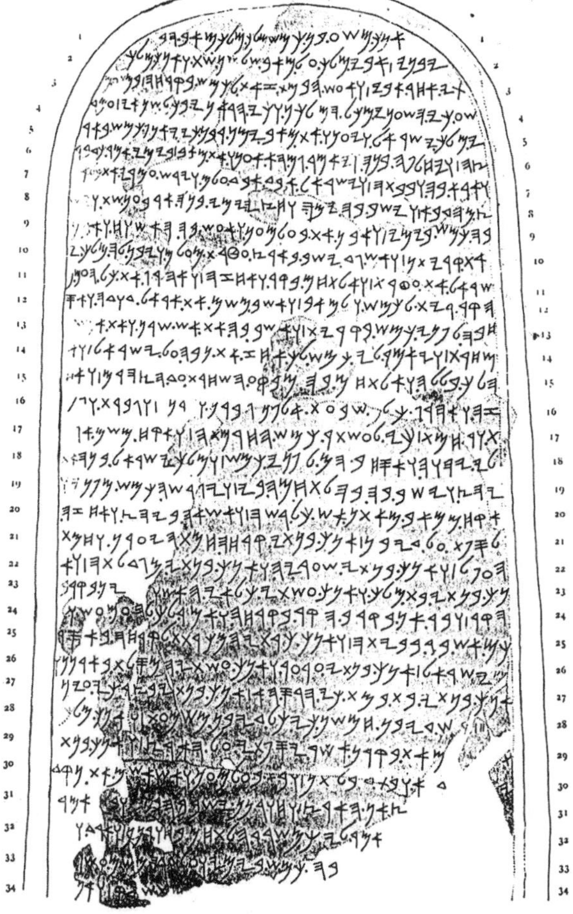

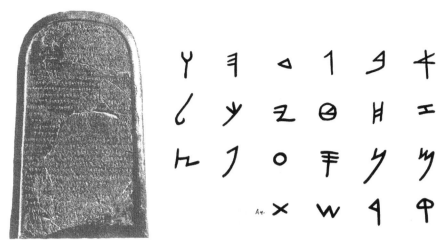

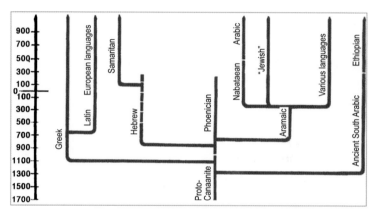

Fig. 3. *The Moabite Mesha stele (c. mid-9th century* BCE*) representing an early phase of the Ancient Hebrew script (above right).*

900
700
500
300
100
0
100
300
500
700
900
1100
1300
1500
1700
Greek
Latin
European languages
Samaritan
Hebrew
Phoenician
Proto-Canaanite
Nabataean
Arabic
"Jewish"
Aramaic
Various languages
Ethiopian
Ancient South Arabic

Fig. 4a. *Alphabet tree.*

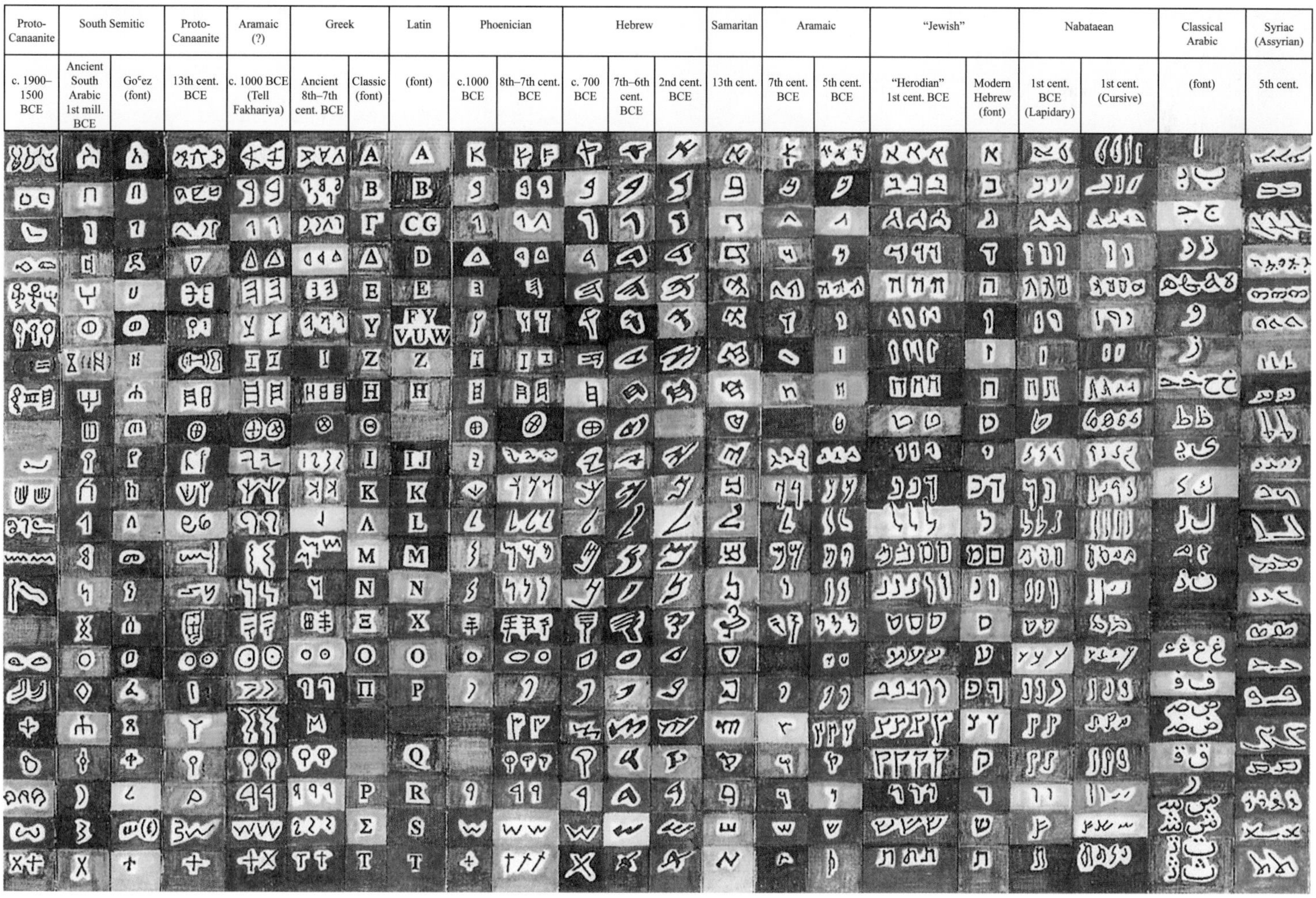

Proto-Canaanite
c. 1900–1500 BCE
South Semitic
Ancient South Arabic 1st mill. BCE
Goʿez (font)
Proto-Canaanite
13th cent. BCE
Aramaic (?)
c. 1000 BCE (Tell Fakhariya)
Greek
Ancient 8th–7th cent. BCE
Classic (font)
Latin
(font)
Phoenician
c.1000 BCE
8th–7th cent. BCE
Hebrew
c. 700 BCE
7th–6th cent. BCE
2nd cent. BCE
Samaritan
13th cent.
Aramaic
7th cent. BCE
5th cent. BCE
"Jewish"
"Herodian" 1st cent. BCE
Modern Hebrew (font)
Nabataean
1st cent. BCE (Lapidary)
1st cent. (Cursive)
Classical Arabic
(font)
Syriac (Assyrian)
5th cent.

Fig. 4b. *Alphabet chart.*

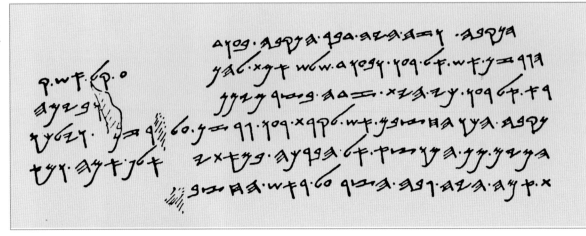

Fig. 5. *The Siloam inscription in Ancient Hebrew letters (end of 8th century* BCE*).*

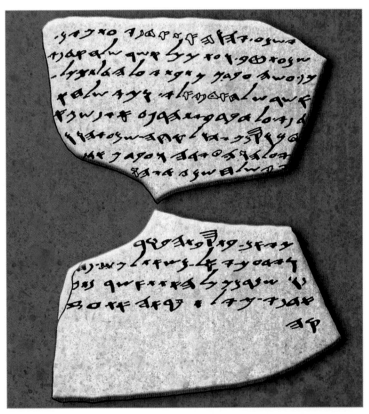

Fig. 6. *An ostracon from Lachish in Ancient Hebrew letters (early 6th century* BCE*).*

those created by the slow carving in hard material. The natural and continuous development of this script seems to have been disturbed at the end of the eighth century BCE, with the expulsion of the northern tribes of Israel, and again, in the early sixth century with the destruction of the First Temple in Jerusalem and the exile of the Judean elite to Babylon. Already in the early sixth century BCE, the ancient Hebrew letters reflecting a *fluent writing in ink* were much shorter, wider, and leaning more backwards than those of the ninth and eighth centuries BCE (figs. 5, 6, 7). While in Babylon, the Jewish scribes who were using the early Hebrew script for writing the Hebrew language became familiar with the *official Aramaic language* and script (figs. 8, 9), which shortly before had become the *lingua franca.* In 539 BCE Babylon fell to Cyrus, king of Persia, and became part of the huge Persian Empire that dominated the countries "from India to Kush (Ethiopia)" (cf. Esther 1:1). Cyrus allowed the exiles to return home. By this time, not only the exiles but many of the people who had remained in Judaea had abandoned the Hebrew language, as evidenced in Nehemiah 13:24: "and their children spake half in the speech of Ashdod and could not speak in the Jews' language." The Persian Empire lasted for about two hundred years, until its defeat by the Macedonian leader, Alexander the Great, in 333 BCE (fig. 10).

Fig. 7. *Ancient Hebrew letters, taken from an ostracon from Arad (early 6th century* BCE*).*

Fig. 8. *Aramaic script of the 5th century* BCE*.*

Fig. 9. *Detail of an Aramaic letter on papyrus, sent by Jews from Egypt to priests in Jerusalem, late 5th century* BCE *(Cowley 30).*

Fig. 10. *Alexander the Great.*

The ancient Hebrew script (Palaeo-Hebrew, to scholars) is attested in Hebrew inscriptions and documents, seals, and bullae from the First Temple period (figs. 5, 6, 11). After the Babylonian conquest of Judaea it seems to have retained a certain measure of eminence, mainly in priestly circles and for religious purposes, and continued to be used by the Jews alongside the Aramaic script. In the Persian and Hellenistic periods Palaeo-Hebraic continued to be used sporadically in Judaea, again mainly in priestly circles and in times of national awakening, such as the Hasmonean period (167–37 BCE) and during the First and Second Revolts against Rome (66–70 CE, 132–135 CE; figs. 12a,b; 13, 14).

In the Book of Ezra, written mainly in Hebrew but which includes letters written in the official Aramaic language of the fifth century BCE, we are told that Ezra was a סופר מהיר, i.e., a skilled scribe, a priest, and learned in the law. The scribe filled an important role in ancient times, when the population was largely illiterate. Close to the temple and to the ruler, he was responsible for the formulation and the writing of official inscriptions, legal documents and letters. Fragments of a fifth-century BCE papyrus scroll with the Aramaic version of the book of Aḥiqar, were found in Elephantine, Egypt (see Porten–Yardeni, 1986–1999, C1.1). Aḥiqar was the advisor and scribe of the Assyrian king Sennacherib (704–681 BCE), called by the latter "the advisor of all Assyria" (col. 1:12), and received from the king his signet-ring (col. 1:3). Aḥiqar is nicknamed ספר חכים ומהיר, "a wise and skilled scribe" (col. 1:1; figs. 15a,b). The Hebrew

Fig. 11. *Ancient Hebrew script on bullae from the City of David (7th century* BCE*).*

9

Fig. 12a. *Ancient Hebrew script on a Hasmonean coin.*

Fig. 12b. *Ancient Hebrew script on a Bar Kokhba coin.*

Fig. 13. *Ancient Hebrew script on a fragment of a monumental inscription from Jerusalem.*

Bible mentions by name about a dozen scribes and some anonymous families of scribes (1 Chr 2:55). Scribes of the clan of Levi (2 Chr 34:13) and of Zebulun (Judg 5:14) are also mentioned, as are "the King's scribe" (2 Kgs 12:11; 2 Chr 24:11) and "the scribes of the King" (Esth 3:12); "the scribe of the commander of the army" (2 Kgs 25:19; Jer 52:25). Even personal items such as "the scribe's chamber" (inside the king's house; Jer 36:12), "the scribe's pen" (Judg 5:14; Ps 45:2), "the scribe's penknife" (Jer 36:23), and "the scribe's inkhorn" (Ezek 9:2, 3) are mentioned. Numerous seals and bullae of scribes have been discovered in Israel and in neighboring countries (fig. 16).

Well known are early statues of Egyptian scribes (from the period of the Fifth Dynasty), clothed only in a short skirt, sitting with legs crossed and holding a papyrus roll

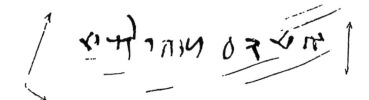

Fig. 14. *Ancient Hebrew script on an ostracon from Masada (no. 457).*

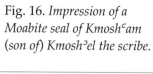

Fig. 16. *Impression of a Moabite seal of Kmoshᶜam (son of) Kmoshʾel the scribe.*

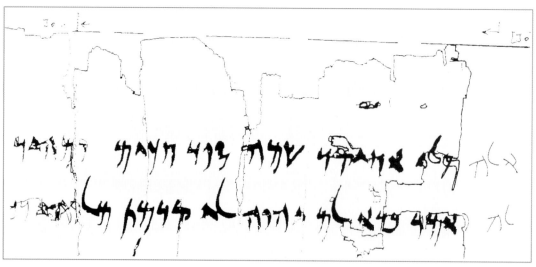

Fig. 15a. *Aḥiqar, a wise and skilled scribe.*

Fig. 15b. *Aḥiqar, the advisor of all Assyria.*

Fig. 18a. *Assyrian and Aramaic scribes on a relief from Nineveh.*

(*from top to bottom*)
Fig. 17a. *Accroupi, an Egyptian scribe of the 5th dynasty.*

Fig. 17b.. *Pes-Shu-Per, Egyptian official posing as scribe (c. 750 BCE).*

Fig. 17c. *Egyptian scribes in a kneeling position.*

Fig. 18b. *Aramaic scribe on a wall painting from Tell Barsip.*

in their left hand and a writing implement (possibly a reed-pen) in their right (figs. 17a,b,c).

Two scribes are depicted on eighth-century BCE Assyrian reliefs, one (an Assyrian scribe) holding a stylus and a clay tablet, and the other (an Aramaic scribe) holding a reed-pen and a papyrus or hide sheet (figs. 18a,b).

Figs. 19a,b,c. *Scribal exercises on Aramaic ostraca from Idumea.*

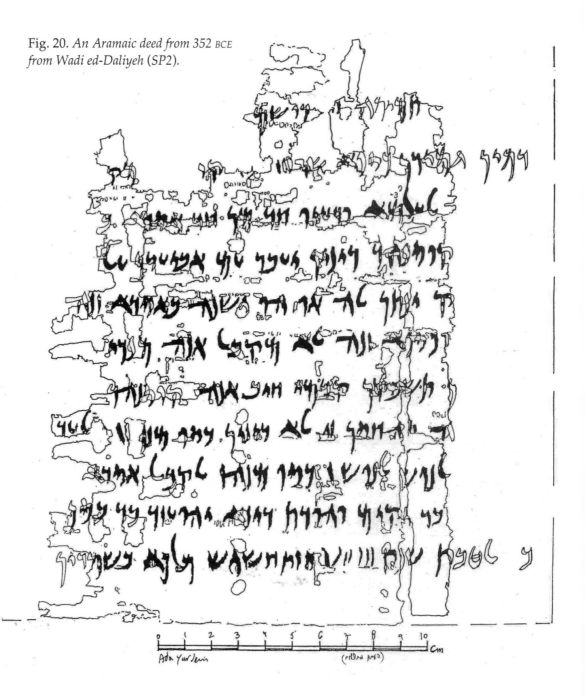

Fig. 20. *An Aramaic deed from 352 BCE from Wadi ed-Daliyeh (SP2).*

The Hebrew and Aramaic words for scribe, as well as for "enumerator", "muster-officer" and "secretary", *sofer* and *safra*, respectively, are perhaps ancient loanwords from Assyrian *šapiru* ("writer" or [perhaps] "ruler"). However, this etymology is not commonly accepted and certain scholars identify these words as West Semitic.

Scribes were taught in schools to formulate texts as well as the art of writing. They learned to use the materials and to form the individual letters in a stylistic, traditional script. Early evidence of the training of scribes was discovered in a library of the high priest of Ugarit; many of the clay tablets found in the building probably were scribal exercises of the pupils. The students would have been chosen from families close to the ruler (Rainey 1969 [Hebrew]; for more information on ancient scribes, see Cohen 2014 [Hebrew]). Scores of clay

12

Fig. 21a. *"Jewish" script on a document from Qumran (Pl. 346).*

Fig. 21b. *"Jewish" script on a document from Qumran (Pl. 377).*

potsherds from the Persian period, mostly covered with ink strokes in the form of half circles, were found among Aramaic ostraca at various sites in the Land of Israel. These, too, were apparently scribal exercises (figs. 19a,b,c).

As evidenced by Aramaic documents from the Persian period found in such countries as India, Bactria, Israel and Egypt, the scribes used an identical Aramaic script style for about two centuries with only minor changes (figs. 20, 9). The official Aramaic script of the fifth to fourth centuries BCE was prevalent throughout the vast Persian Empire, and among the many documents that were discovered mainly in the late nineteenth and early twentieth centuries, was the large collection of Aramaic documents from Elephantine (see Porten and Yardeni 1986–1999).

The situation began to change following the conquest of Persia by Alexander the Great. The division of the Persian Empire into various parts was followed by a process of ramification of the Aramaic script into local script styles. In the Hellenistic period, the individual countries "from India to Nubia" began to develop local script styles based on the official Aramaic script. The various nations that were once part of the Persian Empire continued to use Aramaic for writing their vernaculars, but the forms of the letters changed gradually to such a point that clear differences became evident in the scripts. Documents written in the offshoots of the Aramaic script dating from the late fourth century BCE onward have been discovered in various places of the former Persian Empire. Among other offshoots of the Aramaic script were the so-called "Jewish" script (thus named by F. M. Cross), used by Jews in Judaea, and the "Nabataean" script, the "mother" of Arabic scripts, used by Nabataeans in the region of the Dead Sea, in southern Judaea, and in Sinai (figs. 21a,b; 22).

That most of the epigraphic findings from Judaea are in

the local script that evolved from the cursive Aramaic of the fourth century BCE. The link between the late Aramaic script and its early "Jewish" version, which appears in

Fig. 22. *Detail of a Nabataean deed from Naḥal Ḥever.*

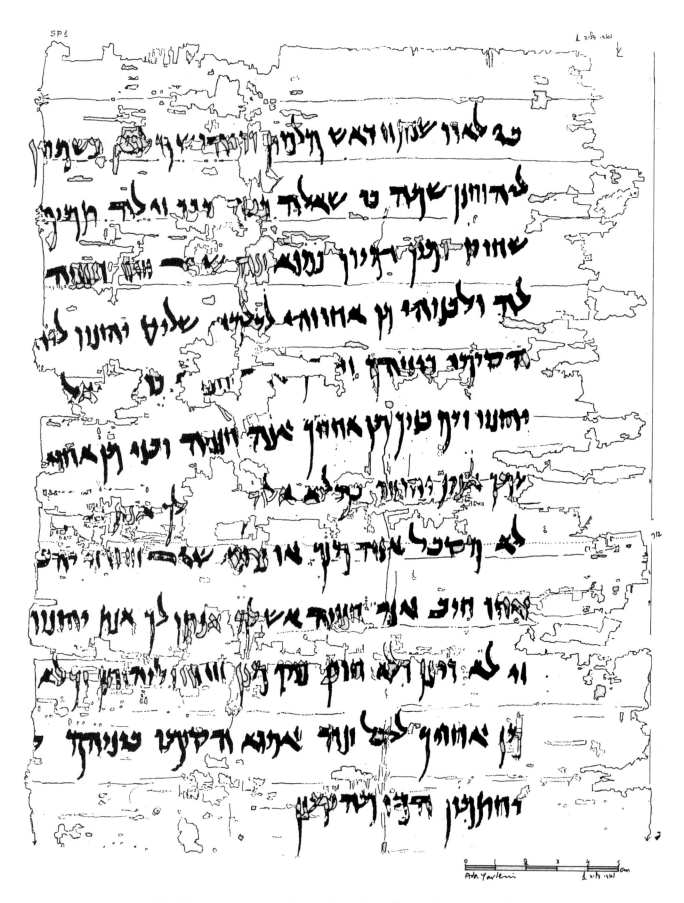

Fig. 23. An Aramaic deed from 335 BCE from Wadi ed-Daliyeh (SP1)

manuscripts from Qumran, is clearly represented by a group of fourth century BCE Aramaic documents (the latest dated 335 BCE) discovered in a cave in Wadi ed-Daliyeh near Jericho (fig. 23); thousands of Aramaic ostraca, also from the fourth century BCE, from Idumea (figs. 24a,b); hundreds of inscriptions discovered on Mount Gerizim, mostly dating from the third and second centuries BCE (fig. 25); and by a dated draft of a marriage contract on an ostracon from Idumea, dated 176 BCE (figs. 26a,b,c). To these, one should add the papyrus document from Egypt (the Nash

⇨ *Continued on p. 17*

Figs. 24a,b. *A 4th century* BCE *Aramaic ostracon from Idumea dated to the second year of Alexander the King (ISAP 1038).*

Fig. 25. *Drawing of a stone inscription from Mt. Gerizim, c. 3rd century* BCE.

Figs. 26a,b,c (*left, below*). *Late Aramaic script on an ostracon from Maresha bearing a draft of an Idumean marriage contract (176* BCE*); drawing, photograph, and alphabetical chart.*

Fig. 27a. *The Nash papyrus, photo: the Ten Commandments and part of* Shema Yisra'el *in a papyrus fragment from Egypt from about the mid-2nd century* BCE *(Cambridge University Library, Or. 233).*

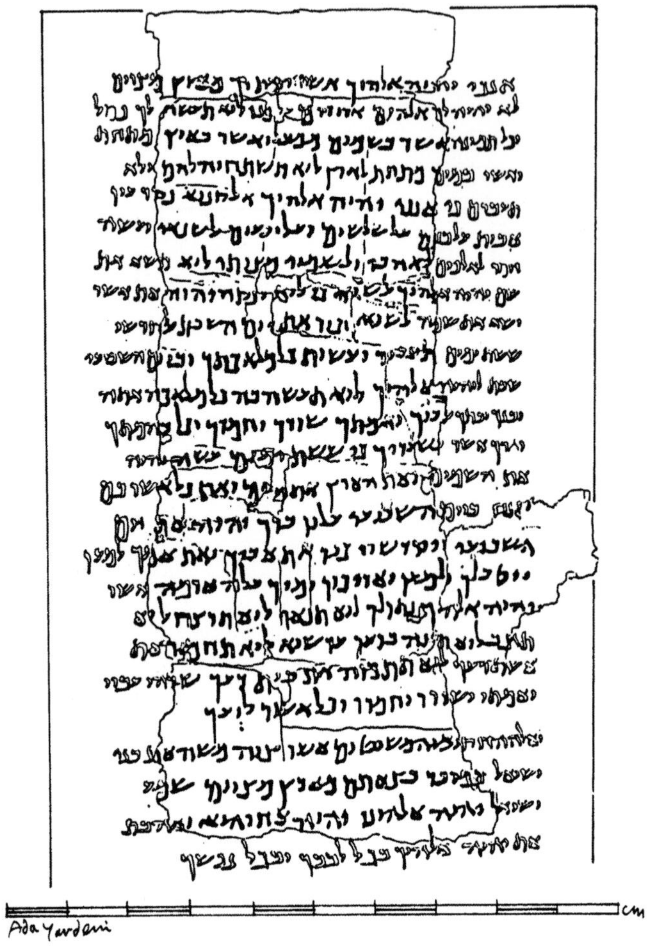

Fig. 27b. *The Nash papyrus, drawing with restored text.*

Fig. 28a. *A deed on papyrus from "year four of the destruction of the House of Israel."*

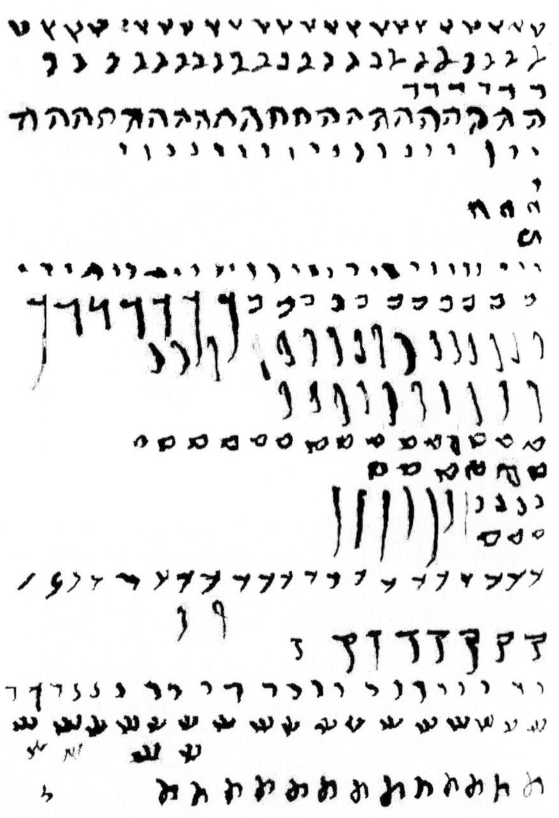

Fig. 28b. *An alphabetical chart of the deed of "year four of the destruction of the House of Israel."*

Fig. 27c. *The Nash papyrus, alphabetical chart.*

Papyrus; figs. 27a,b,c), with the Ten Commandments and part of "*Shema*" written in a semi-cursive, "pre-Jewish" script from about the mid-second century BCE (this script somewhat resembles that of the Maresha ostracon [fig. 26]). All these assist in the approximate dating of the early documents in the "Jewish" script.

The most important discovery of documents from this time written in the "Jewish" script is still the discovery of the documents from the Judean Desert, mainly those known as the Dead Sea Scrolls, dating from the late third century BCE to the end of the Bar Kokhba Revolt, in 135/6 CE (a document from "the 4th year of the destruction of the House of Israel" [figs. 28a,b] can probably be dated to 140 CE). However, not only the "Jewish" script appears in these documents but also a later version of the Palaeo-Hebrew script used in the Second Temple period. About a dozen biblical scrolls found at Qumran dating from approximately the second and first centuries BCE, are written in the early Hebrew script (fig. 29). In addition, the *tetragrammaton* and the divine name *El* occasionally appear in the Palaeo-Hebrew script in scrolls otherwise written in the "Jewish" script (fig. 30). (Also found in the Judean Desert caves were many documents written in Greek letters but these will not be discussed here.)

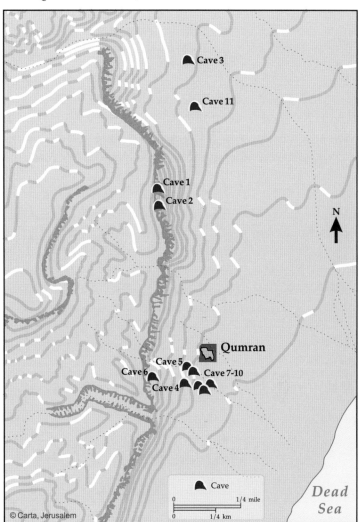

Fig. 29. *Ancient Hebrew letters taken from fragments of a Leviticus scroll from Qumran*

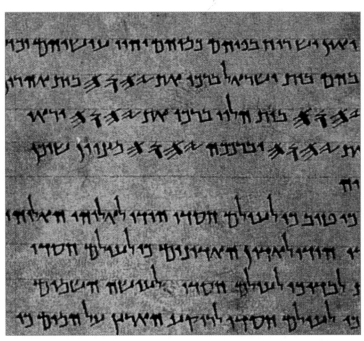

Fig. 30. *A detail of a Psalms scroll from Qumran (11Q Ps.) with the divine name in Palaeo-Hebrew letters (photo: Israel Antiquities Authority).*

Palaeography as a Tool in the Reading and Dating of the Dead Sea Scrolls

The Dead Sea Scrolls consist of about 900 different compositions, some of which are attested in more than one copy. Produced by scores of scribes and copyists over almost three centuries, they show the graphic evolution of the so-called "Jewish" letter-forms during this period.

Palaeography (the study of ancient writing) deals with *the formal evolution of the letter signs*. The Hebrew alphabet contains 22 conventional graphic signs representing 23 consonants, five of which have a variant form when appearing at the end of a word (making it 27 different signs). Ask several people to write the first letter of the Hebrew alphabet, meaning the letter Alef, in the modern Hebrew script style, and the results will vary in detail from one person to another, even though all of them would use *a similar writing instrument on a similar writing surface*. The differences will be in *size*, in the *form*, in the *direction of the strokes*, and in *their meeting points with each other*. Despite these differences, we would be able to identify the letter as Alef, and distinguish it from other letters in the Hebrew alphabet, such as Bet, because all these people use a *common script style*. In this style, each letter has a *limited number of basic strokes* (e.g., 3 for Alef, 3 for Bet, 2 for Gimel, 2 for Dalet, and so on), which may be called the "root" of the letter (fig. 31). To assure that various letters with an equal number of basic strokes will not look alike (e.g., Bet and Kaf, Gimel and Nun, Dalet and Resh), each two strokes have *a limited range of meeting points with each other*, as well as *a limited range of directions*. One should distinguish between *stylistic features* and *personal features* of a handwriting. Thus, the *size* of the letters, the *precise angle of their tilt*, and, to a certain extent, *the form of the individual strokes*, not only reflect the writer's skill and training, but also his character, age and his mental and physical condition, albeit the latter of which lie in the realm of graphology rather than palaeography. In order to identify a script sign in a written text, we usually *ignore the personal factor* and relate only to the *conventional basic forms of the letters* in the script style used by the writer. The ability of the human brain to perceive only the conventional forms of the script, while ignoring its personal features enabled people to communicate with each other in writing.

The formal changes occurring in each letter over the course of time result from several factors. These include *technical elements*, such as the *type and shape of the writing tools and materials*, the *manner and the angle of holding the writing implement*, and the *speed of writing*. The *influence of other script styles* or *artistic fashions* is also a common occurrence causing changes in the forms of the letter signs. In addition, a *deliberate change* in the form of the letter-signs through *imitation* of given forms, or the *creation of new forms*, may also take place. When a change prevails within a certain group of people, in a certain place, at a certain period of time, this change may be regarded as a *stylistic change*.

In order to determine these changes in a certain handwriting, the palaeographer examines the *structure* of the letter-sign, its *various strokes*—the *basic ones as well as the additional components*, the *number of the strokes*, their *relative size and thickness*, their *directions*, their *meeting points with each other*, and *the order in which they were drawn* in the particular letter-sign (figs. 32, 33, 34, 35).

The palaeographer also measures the average *width* and

Fig. 31. *The "roots" of the Hebrew letters.*

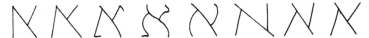

Fig. 32. *Various forms of Alef.*

height of the letters, the *relative size* of different letters, and the spacing between letters as well as the space between the rows of script. The results are then compared to other handwritings of the same or of another group, in order to detect the *different features* (for identifying an *individual scribe*) or the *common features* (for identifying a *common style*). Thus, palaeographic examination can assist in the classification and dating of inscriptions and manuscripts according to their style, and in identifying individual scribes. One should bear in mind that *most of the ancient epigraphic material is undated*, a fact which leaves a wide gamut for speculation and often causes disputes among scholars, who date it in favor of their historical views.

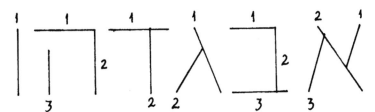

Fig. 33. *The basic strokes in different letters.*

Although palaeography alone cannot supply a definite dating, it can determine a *relative chronology based on a sequence of formal changes* which have occurred in the letter-signs in the course of time.

As one letter may appear in many variant forms in different documents and even in the same document, the variant forms of the letters may be classified into several prominent types, which may be distinguished according to four criteria:

1. Stylistic differences which reflect different traditions or different schools of scribes;
2. The distinction between calligraphic and cursive types of one and the same script style;
3. The distinction between early and late forms of the letters;
4. The distinction between the form of the letter in medial and final position in the word.

In the fourth and third centuries BCE, it is often hard to attribute a particular letter-form to one of the above four criteria. As noted, this was a period of transition which witnessed the weakening of the Aramaic official tradition, the appearance of the first representatives of its derivatives, and the appearance of many variant forms of each letter. The extant documents show a complex situation in which different types of letters appear together (see Yardeni, 1991b).

There are differences between the earlier and later manuscripts among the Dead Sea scrolls and between those written by different hands. In general, *the number of different hands equals the number of copyists or scribes*, most of whom used one and the same script, i.e., the so-called "Jewish" script.

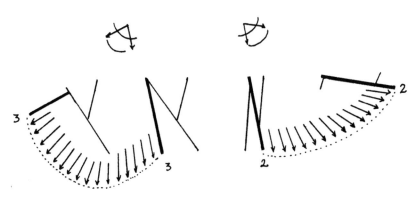

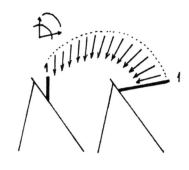

Fig. 34 (*left*). *The range of directions of the three basic strokes of Alef.*

Fig. 35 (*below*). *Meeting-points of the three basic strokes of Alef.*

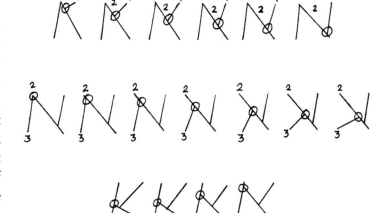

The graphic development of the letters does not always fit the chronological order of the documents. There are, on the one hand, the first occurrences of a late form in early documents and, on the other hand, archaic forms in late documents. Each letter has its own pace of evolution and that pace varies from place to place. Therefore, undated documents may be dated only approximately and not absolutely. Chronology aside, when several stages in the development of the letter-form are documented, it is usually possible to describe the graphic evolution of the letter-forms and determine a relative chronology (see Yardeni 2000, vol. B, Palaeography).

Toward the Birth of the "Jewish" Script

The Aramaic script of the late fourth to the second centuries BCE (fig. 36) has many affinities with the script in the earliest scroll fragments from Qumran, and mainly the fragments of 4QSam[b] (figs. 37a,b,c). The dating of the many (undated)

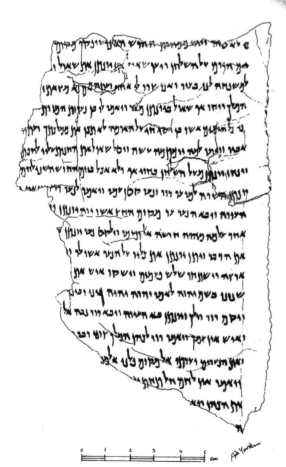

(*counterclockwise, from left*)
Fig. 37a. *4QSam[b], late 3rd century* BCE. (*photo: Israel Antiquities Authority*).

Fig. 37b. *Drawing of 4QSam[b].*

Fig. 37c. *Alphabetical chart of 4QSam[b], late 3rd century* BCE.

documents in Aramaic script from this period which were found in Egypt and in Israel is based on palaeographical and historical criteria. A papyrus document from Egypt that bears many Greek names (fig. 38) may be dated to the second half of the third century BCE. The script on an ostracon from Edfu (fig. 39) has many affinities with the script of the fragments of the 4QJer[a] Scroll (figs. 40a,b,c). The Sam[b] and the Jer[a] fragments, as well as a few short inscriptions discovered on Mount Gerizim (fig. 25) may be regarded as a link between the Aramaic and the "Jewish" scripts. Their script still resembles the late Aramaic script, yet it also has many affinities with the "Jewish" script in its early phases. As none of the Qumran documents published until now bears a date, there is a gap of more than two hundred years between the latest dated document in the Aramaic script found so far (the Maresha ostracon dating from 176 BCE (fig. 26) and the earliest dated document in the "Jewish" script (pap. Mur. 18 [written in the "Jewish" cursive script style]) dated to the second year of Caesar Nero (55/56 CE; fig. 41).

Fig. 36. *Alphabet taken from a 4th century* BCE *Aramaic deed from Wadi ed-Daliyeh (SP1).*
The arrows indicate the supposed direction of the strokes.

Fig. 38. *An Aramaic document from Egypt (pap. Levi della Vida) with Greek names (c. 3rd century* BCE*).*

Fig. 39. *Final Lamed in an Aramaic*
ostracon from Edfu, Egypt,
dating from the 3rd century BCE.

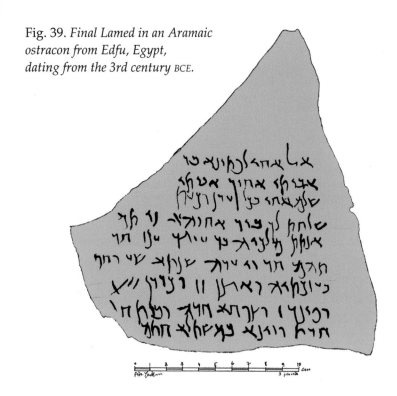

Fig. 41. *A deed on papyrus dating from 55/56* CE, *written in the cursive*
"Jewish" script.

Fig. 40a. *Detail of 4QJer^a (late 3rd or early 2nd century BCE): photo.*

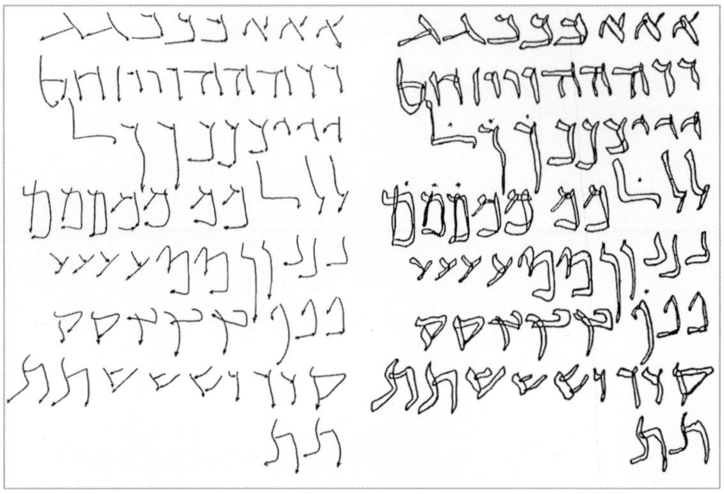

Fig. 40c. *Alphabetical chart of 4QJer^a (late 3rd or early 2nd century BCE).*

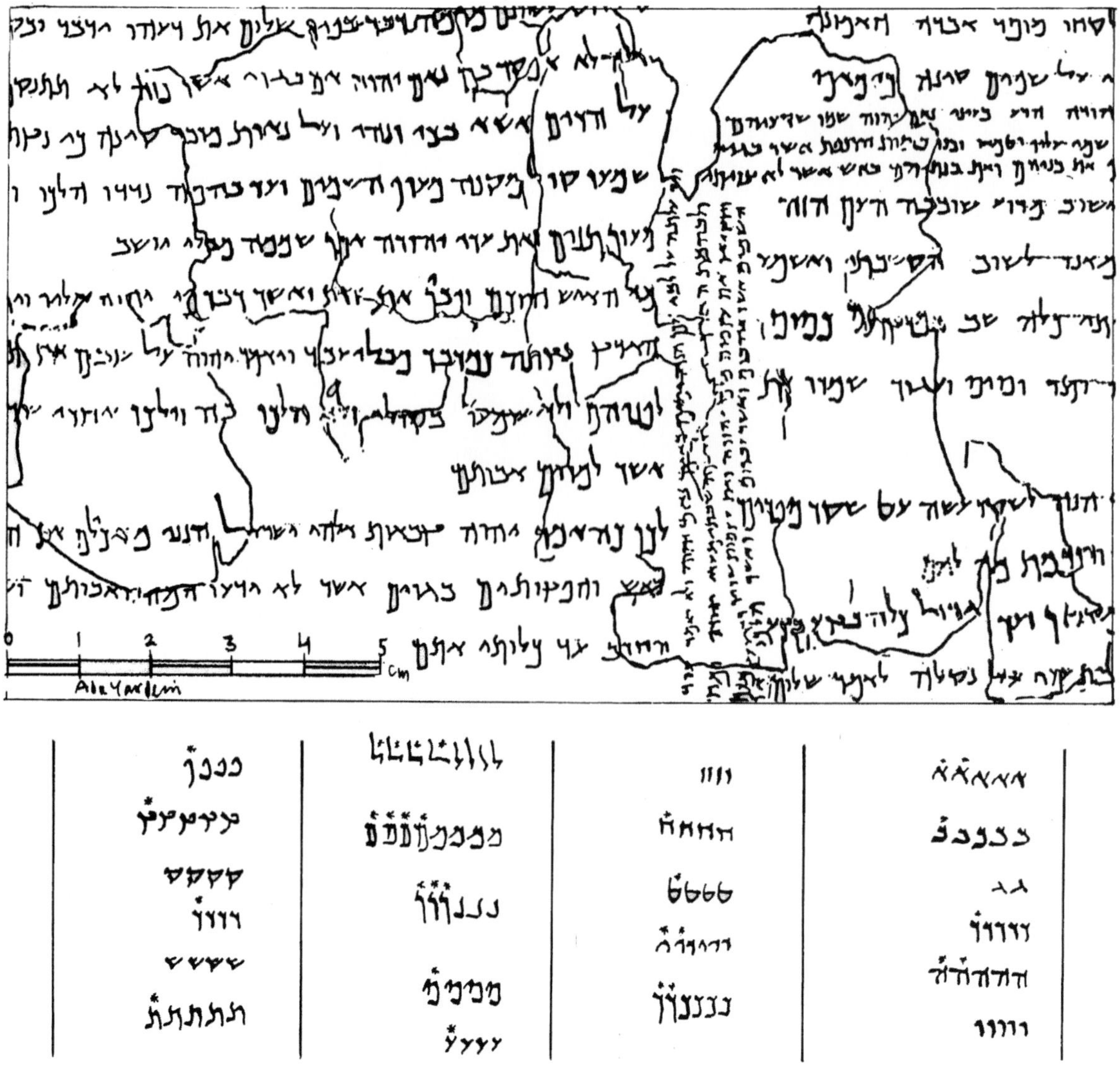

Fig. 40b. *Detail of 4QJer^a (late 3rd or early 2nd century BCE): drawing.*

Prominent Characteristics of Certain Late Aramaic and Early "Jewish" Letters

Already in the late Aramaic script, medial and final forms of certain letters began to appear, as well as different formal types of individual letters (fig. 42). Both characteristics prevail in the "Jewish" script, while the *different types of letter-forms* prevail mainly in the cursive hand. To these belong, among others, the *looped Alef* (fig. 43), the extreme cursive Bet, the tripod-type of He, the two-strokes-type of Waw, the comma-type of Yod, the wavy-stroke-type of Lamed, the circle-and down-stroke-type of Mem, the backward-curved type of Nun, as well as its extreme cursive form, and the looped Taw. Already in the late Aramaic script, curved strokes began to straighten out and, as a result, angular joins are formed (fig. 23). This *square appearance of the script* is one of the defining features of the "Jewish" book-hand. Another feature of the early "Jewish" book-hand is the regularity of the writing, resulting from the suspension of the letters on straight guide-lines (not attested in Aramaic documents written in ink). At this early stage of independent development, the letters in the "Jewish" script were not yet adorned with flourishes, except for the inherited serifs in several letters, such as Bet, Dalet, Kaf, Mem, Qof, and Resh. The distinction between thick horizontal strokes and thin vertical strokes, characteristic of the late Aramaic script (see, e.g., the Wadi ed-Daliyeh papyri [fig. 23]), is still attested in the earliest documents from Qumran (e.g., 4QSam[b] [fig. 37]), and occasionally even in later documents, but is not typical of the "Jewish" script. The process of splitting into different script-styles, i.e., the book-hand and the cursive hand, already began in the early stages of evolution of the "Jewish" script, but did not crystallize until the early first century CE.

Fig. 42 (right). Medial and final forms of letters in the late Aramaic script on an ostracon from Edfu, Egypt.

Fig. 43. *"Looped" Alef and Taw in the 4th century BCE Aramaic script.*

Main Phases in the Evolution of the "Jewish" Script

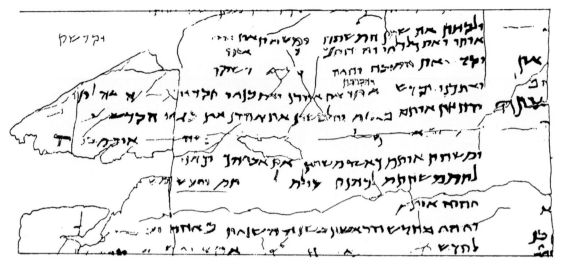

Only a small number out of the many Qumran texts allude to historical events by which their composition may be dated (however, some of these texts may have been copied later). The prominent surveys dealing with the palaeographical aspects of the Qumran documents are those of Frank Moore Cross, Jr. (1955, 1961), and Nahman Avigad (1961). A few scholars tried to follow in their steps, by just dealing with a particular manuscript or with a group of manuscripts. Until now, no complete palaeographic research of the Dead Sea Scrolls has been attempted. Following Cross, we count *three main phases* in the evolution of the "Jewish" script. Most of the documents from Qumran represent the first and second phases (here b and c) while some fragments belong to an earlier phase termed "*pre-Jewish*" (here a).

The phases are as follows:

a. *The pre-Jewish phase* (from the late third century BCE until the Hasmonean revolt in 167 BCE). Best known are the Enoch fragments (4Q201), the 4QSam[b] fragments, the

Figs. 45a,b. Detail of 4QEx[f] written in a cursive pre-"Jewish" script: drawing (above) and alphabetical chart (below).

Fig. 44. *Detail of the 4Q201 Enoch scroll from Qumran, c. late 3rd century BCE (photo: Israel Antiquities Authority).*

4QJer[a] fragments, and the 4QEx[f] fragments (figs. 44, 37, 40, 45a,b, respectively) from Qumran, as well as the above-mentioned Nash papyrus (fig. 27).

b. *The Hasmonean phase* (167–37 BCE). The famous Isaiah Scroll (1QIsa[a]) belongs palaeographically to about the middle of this period (figs. 46a,b,c). See also a fragment of an early scroll of Tobit (fig. 47), and the Habakkuk Commentary scroll (fig. 48), from the late Hasmonean period.

c. *The Herodian phase* (37 BCE to the destruction of the Second Temple in 70 CE). The Psalms Scroll (11Q5) belongs palaeographically to this phase (figs. 30, 49a,b, 50, 51).

24

⇨ *Continued on p. 27*

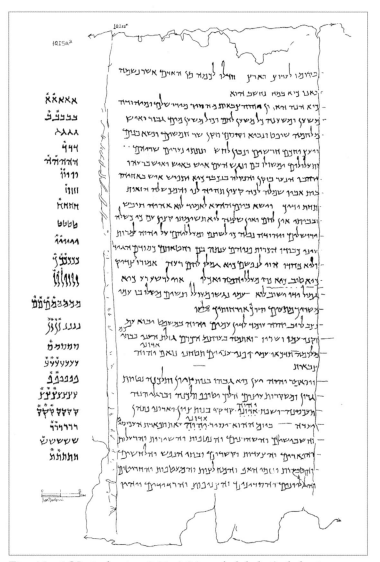

Fig. 46a. *1QIsaᵃ, chapters 2:21–3:24, and alphabetical chart.*

Fig. 46b. *1QIsaᵃ, synthetic, average forms of the letters in col. XLII, enlarged and placed on rectangles for a palaeographic description.*

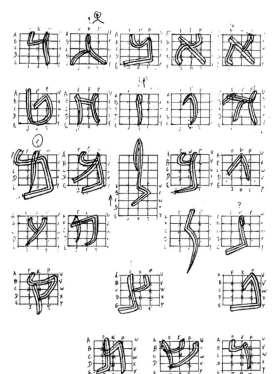

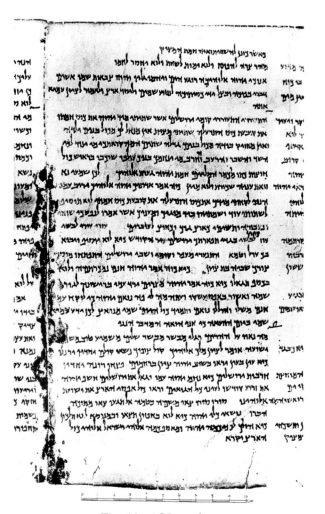

Fig. 46c. *1QIsaᵃ: photo.*

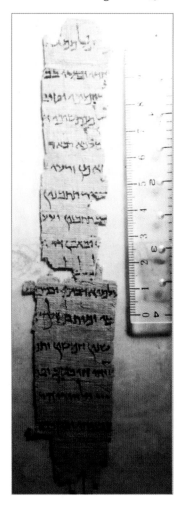

Fig. 47. *Fragment of a Tobit scroll (Tobitᵃʳ·ᵃ, 4Q196) in an early "Jewish" script of about the late 2nd or early 1st century* BCE.

25

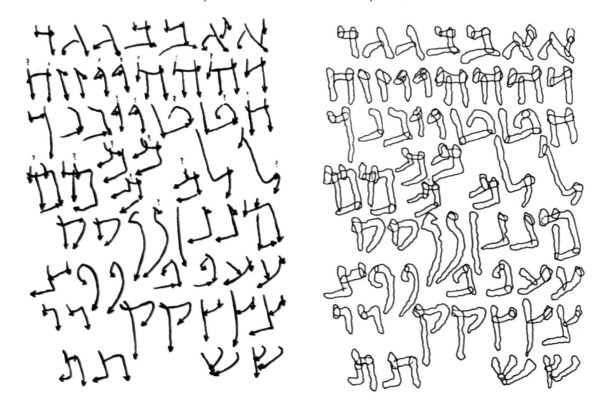

ותתם טימו אים וחמס שיא קריה ועל וישבי בה
פשר הדבר על הכוהן הרשע לשלם לו את X
גמ לו אשר גבל על אביונים טמא לבון הוא
עצת היחד ותבדמת הממך קטא ותורה עישה
התורה אשר ושופטנו אל בתוך
כאשר זמם לכלות אביונים יאשר אמר מימי
קריה וחמס ארץ פשר הקריה הוא וירושלם
תרש''ע
אשר פעל בה הכוהן מעשות תעגות ויטמא את
מקדש אל וחמס ארץ המה עירי והודה אשר
על חין אביונ'ם מד הועיל כסל טא כל וצרי
מו בה ומרו שקר טוא בטחו ועד וערו עלוהו
לעשות אלולים אלם פשר הדבר על כל על
כסלי הגוים אשר יצרום לעוברם ולא תשחת
לחטז והמה לוא יצילום ביום המשפט הנה חיו
ונטי ויתד ר'ם

Fig. 48. *Detail and alphabet taken from the Habakkuk Commentary scroll from Qumran*
from about the late Hasmonean period.

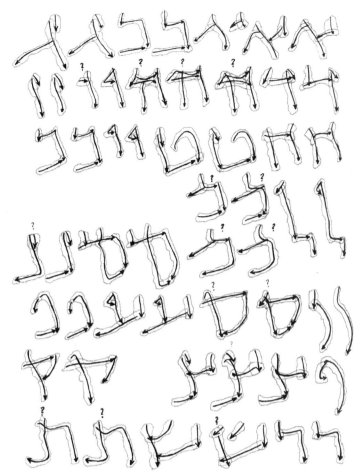

Fig. 49a. *Analysis of enlarged letter-forms with additional flourishes of the Herodian period taken from the Psalms Scroll from Qumran (11Q5). The arrows designate the directions of the strokes.*

styles, and even round semi-formal styles, etc. These characteristics may complicate a simple distinction between the various phases of evolution of the letter-forms. To be able to distinguish between these characteristics and the prominent features of a script in a certain period of time, the palaeographer must be familiar with the prominent features that mark the evolution of the letter-forms.

An untrained eye should look for the *most prominent features* in each phase. Thus, the *tendency to balance the height of the letters* and the increase in the number of *independent ornamental components* mark the beginning of the Herodian period. Additions, such as small strokes or a thickening at the tops of certain letters, may vary. This means that manuscripts written in the *book-hand* which *lack these flourishes* are presumed to be earlier. However, in rapid writing these additions may have been omitted, while *with time some additions became integral parts of the letter-signs*, altering the forms of the letters.

d. *The post-Herodian phase* (70 CE to the end of the Bar Kokhba revolt in 135 CE). Qumran was already destroyed by this time. While rich in documentary texts, written in the cursive hand, the book-hand of this phase is poorly attested.

A few fragments of biblical scrolls found in caves of the Judean desert, mainly Wadi Murrabaʿat and Naḥal Ḥever, belong to this phase. These include fragments of Genesis and of Exodus from Wadi Murrabaʿat (figs. 52, 53) as well as a fragment of a Psalms scroll from Naḥal Ḥever (figs. 54a,b), and some of the Bar Kokhba letters and deeds (figs. 55a,b,c).

The *arbitrary distinction* between the phases was meant to facilitate the palaeographic description but refers to *historical rather than palaeographical periods*. In fact, the *change in the letter-forms is an ongoing process with a living script*. The changes are *gradual*, each letter having its own pace of evolution. The dating is therefore based on the comparison of the letter-forms in different handwritings, thus offering only a *relative chronology*.

In his detailed analysis of the "Jewish" scripts, Cross distinguishes between several script-styles which may have existed together, mainly the formal, cursive and vulgar styles as well as semi-formal and semi-cursive

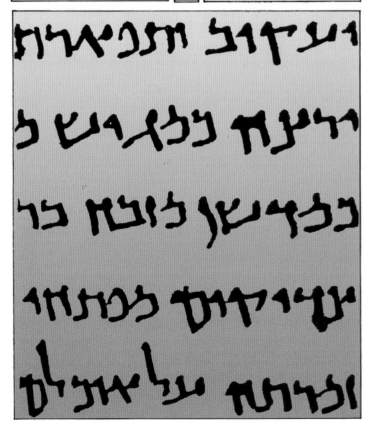

Fig. 49b. *Details (clockwise from top left) of the War Scroll, the Thanksgiving Scroll and the Psalms Scroll from Qumran written in the Herodian "Jewish" script.*

In the post-Herodian period, the height of the letters became more even and the flourishes became an integral feature of the letters.

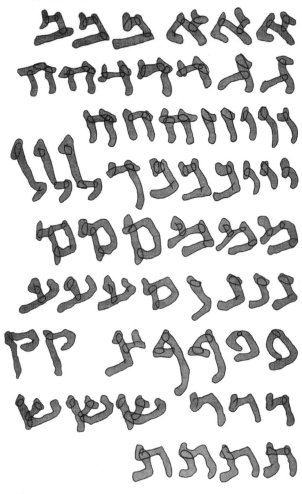

(*counterclockwise from upper left*)

Fig. 50. *A formal, late Hasmonean or early Herodian script-style with personal features of a professional scribe, in a fragment of 4QMMT (4Q397).*

Fig. 51. *An early Herodian book-hand, taken from the Qumran War Scroll.*

Fig. 52. *Fragments of an Exodus scroll from Wadi Murraba‘at (Mur. Plate 824; late 1st or early 2nd century* CE*).*

Fig. 53. *A post-Herodian book-hand, taken from the Genesis scroll fragments from Wadi Murabba‘at.*

Figs. 54a,b. *Fragment of a Psalms scroll from Naḥal Ḥever (NH 41), c. 1st century* CE; *photograph (above) and drawing (below).*

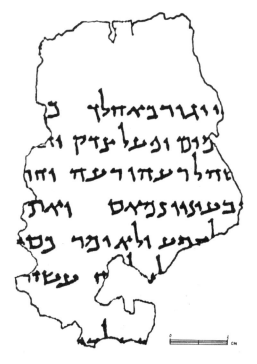

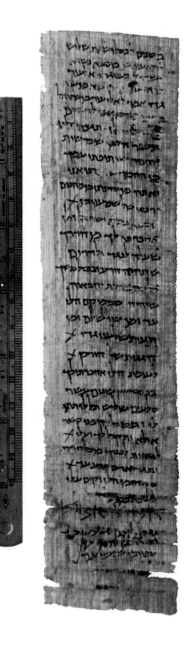

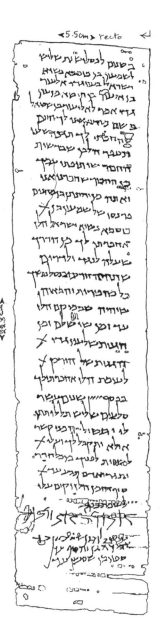

Figs. 55a,b *(above right). A dated Hebrew deed in an elegant "Jewish" book-hand on papyrus from Naḥal Ḥever (P. Yadin 45), 134* CE: *photograph and drawing.*

Fig. 55c *(right). Detail and alphabet taken from P. Yadin 45, 134* CE.

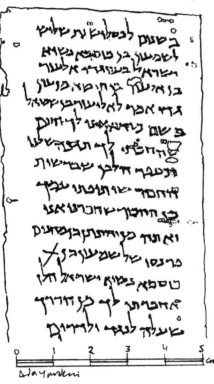

Morphological Aspect of the Letters

In order to be able to describe the form of a letter, one has to analyze its basic components. The task is easy when a script was made with a sharp instrument matching the skeleton of the letter (figs. 56a,b). If, on the other hand, a flat nib was used (fig. 57), the skeleton may be hidden but can be exposed by tracing the central axis of each stroke,

gradually changed into local variants. Different cursive scripts evolved from the traditional book-hand style, and the varying styles each influenced the other. The changes in the book-hand style were relatively slow, thanks to the dictated instructions for the writing of Torah scrolls. But as political events continued to influence the Hebrew script,

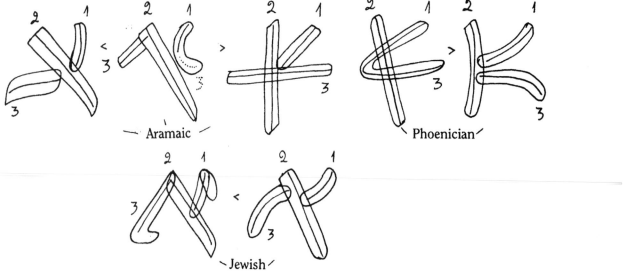

Fig. 56a. *Basic strokes of Alef in the Phoenician, Aramaic and Jewish scripts.*

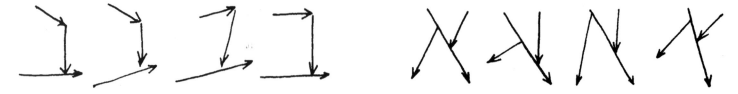

Fig. 56b. *The three basic strokes of Alef and Bet differing in their directions and in their meeting points.*

provided one is familiar with the morphology of the letter. The palaeography of the "Jewish" script is the study of the morphology of the letter-forms used in Judaea from about the third century BCE to about 135 (or 140?) CE, the year of the latest dated documents found in the Judean Desert.

The flourishes to the letters of the "Jewish" script evolved naturally until the time when rules for the writing of Torah scrolls were established. These rules included the description of the structure of the letters according to their forms at the time the guidelines were set. Following the migration of the Jews from Judaea and their dispersion in various countries, the precise forms of the Hebrew letters

the scribal tradition slackened and the verbal instructions, without definite examples of the traditional forms, became more vague.

Three main phenomena may be noticed in the development of the "Jewish" script of the Second Temple period: 1) the development of medial and final forms of the letters; 2) the leveling of the height of the letters; and 3) the development of flourishes in individual letters, including the group of the seven letters Gimel, Zayin, Tet, Nun, Ayin, Tsadi, and Shin, which, by analogy, gradually developed similar additional strokes. This group is not mentioned in the Mishnah but appears in the Talmud.

Fig. 57. *A flat nib creates strokes that may hide the skeleton of the letter.*

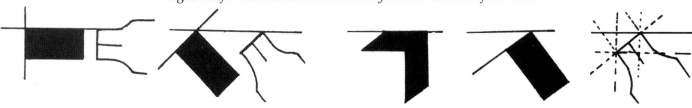

Fig. 58a. *A Byzantine letter on papyrus (Ms.Heb*f *114), c. 5th or 6th century* CE.

Fig. 58b. *Changes in the form of the additional flourishes in the seven letters—Gimel, Zayin, Tet, Nun, Ayin, Tsadi, and Shin (Sha*c*atnez Gets).*

The Talmud (*Menaḥot* 29) refers to Rabbi Akiva son of Joseph (early second century CE), as the person who "was going to preach on each tip of the letters piles upon piles of rules." In the same place the Talmud tells of Rava (son of Joseph son of Hama [280–355 CE]), who was the head of the Makhoza Yeshivah in the fourth century CE, that he explicitly mentioned that "seven letters need three *ziyunin*—Sha^catnez Gets" (an acronym of Shin, Ayin, Tet, Nun, Zayin, Gimel, Tsadi). The word *ziyunin* refers to either "ornaments" or to the letter Zayin, and was later interpreted as three small Zayin signs which should be added at the top of each of these seven letters. However, in documents and mosaics of the fifth to seventh centuries, an identical addition was appended to the top of the single or the left down-stroke of these seven letters, which was made with a to-and-fro stroke (the best example appears in a papyrus document from Egypt now in Oxford [Ms. Heb^f114]; see Yardeni 1997, pp. 76 and 179; figs. 58a,b). This, in the writer's opinion, is the original ornamet referred to by Rava (the to-and-fro stroke later became a cross-like ornament which gradually turned into a rhombus and then to a short horizontal stroke at the top of the down-stroke). The first stages in the development of these and other additional strokes to the letters may be traced back to the early stages of the so-called "Jewish" script, as it evolved from the Aramaic official script after the fall of the Persian Empire. In addition to the three main

phenomena mentioned above, certain prominent features in individual letters appeared, such as the closing of the gap at the left lower corner of Samekh and final Mem, and the extension of the base-stroke of Bet to the right beyond its meeting point with the down-stroke. These changes took place during the first century BCE, i.e., the late Hasmonean and the early Herodian periods.

1QIsa^a is an example of the Hasmonean handwriting from about the early first century BCE (fig. 46). Almost no flourishes are added to the basic forms of the letters except for the independent stroke slanting to the left at the top of Waw, Yod, and Lamed, and except for the "serifs" (the protrusion at the top of the "roof" of the letter, created by the writing implement when it touches the writing surface when first producing the letter-form) inherited from the Aramaic mother-script (fig. 8). However, the tops of Nun, Zayin and Gimel start to bend backwards, thus heralding in the seven-letter group "Sha^catnez Gets" (see above). Other characteristics of the 1QIsa^a scroll are the open Samekh and the letters Kaph, Mem, Pe and Tsadi, the medial forms of which still extend below the imaginary baseline, reflecting the original forms of these letters, having long "legs" in the Aramaic script and later appearing in medial and final variants.

The prayer for King Jonathan (figs. 59a,b,c), otherwise known as Alexander Jannaeus (103–76 BCE), dated on

Fig. 59a. *Mixed script in the prayer for King Jonathan (4Q448).*

historical and palaeographical data to the first quarter of the first century BCE, exhibits a variety of more or less cursive letter-forms, such as three forms of Mem and two forms of Lamed. It also shows early and later forms of one and the same letter, such as an open (early) and a closed (late) form of Samekh, a semi-cursive Kaf in medial and final position, and Waw and Yod adorned with a triangular loop instead of the former "hook".

A large amount of epigraphic material survives from the Herodian period. In addition to the Qumran documents, there are many burial and ossuary inscriptions, as well as ostraca. The Masada finds belong to the end of this period. A significant increase in ornamental elements in the letters, in the form of independent additional strokes, is attested in the Herodian period (fig. 48). Characteristics of this peiod also include the leveling of the height of the letter-forms and the crystallization of different script styles, such as the calligraphic book-hand, which later developed into the elegant script of Torah scrolls, and the standard cursive script style that prevailed in Judaea during the late Herodian and post-Herodian periods. The

cursive script, which evolved from the book-hand style, developed gradually yet rapidly over the period of two centuries (from the mid-second century BCE to about the mid-first century CE), and the reading of its extreme forms requires special training, unlike the beautiful book-hand of most of the Qumran scrolls, the script of which is lucid for readers of modern Hebrew.

Some examples of different script styles from the Herodian period include: the book-hand style in the Psalms Scroll (figs. 49a,b); representative script carved in stone in an inscription from Jerusalem (fig. 60); a mixed script on the epitaph of King Uzziah (fig. 61); incised script on ossuaries from the time of the loop-fashion (fig. 62); a semi-cursive hand in scroll fragments of Enoch manuscript g (4Q212; fig. 63); and a cursive script-style on ostraca from Masada (fig. 64). Many dated documents from the late

Fig. 59b. *Palaeographic comparative chart of 4Q448.*

Lower Columns (B and C)			Upper Column (A)		
Cursive	Semi-cursive	Book-hand	Cursive	Semi-cursive	Book-hand
	אאאא		א	אא	
	בבבבבב			בב	ב
י		יי			י
ה	דדד	דדד	ד	ד	דדד
וווי	ו	ווווו		ו	ווווווו
	וו				
וווווו	ווי		וו	ו	וווווו
בבבבבג	בבבבבבבב	בב			ב
ןןןןןן					ןןןןן
ססססססססססססס	ססססססססססס	סססססס	ססססס	ס	סססס
ן	ןן				ל
ן					
	ם	ם		ם	ם
ע	עעעעע			עעע	
	פ			פ	
				צ	
	קקקק				
ךךךד	ררר	ררר	ר	ררר	ר
	ששששששש שש	ש		שש	
תתתתתת	תתתתתת		תת		

0 1 2 3 4 5

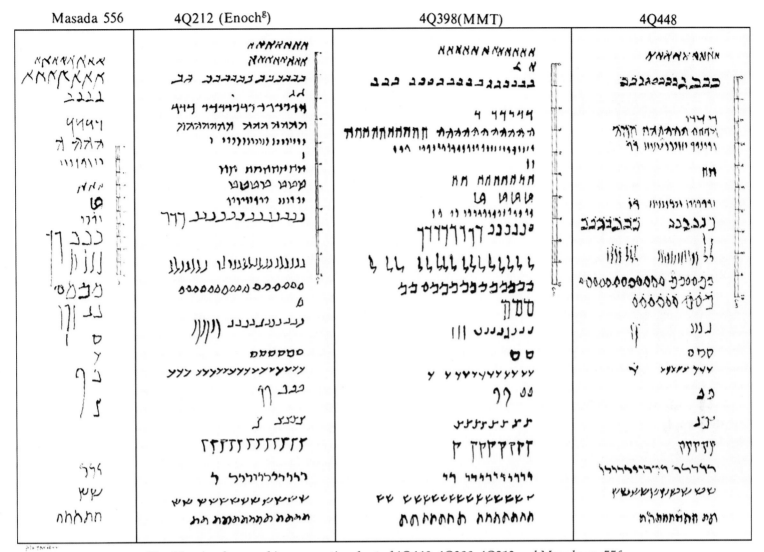

Fig. 59c. *A palaeographic comparative chart of 4Q448, 4Q398, 4Q212 and Masada no. 556.*

Fig. 60. *Carved letters in a stone inscription from Jerusalem.*

Herodian and post-Herodian periods have been found, mainly in the Wadi Murabbaᶜat and Naḥal Ḥever caves, the earliest dating to 55/56 CE (Mur. 18; fig. 41), written in the "Jewish" cursive script. Many different hands, in more or less cursive styles, appear in the documents from the post-Herodian period. The Jewish book-hand reached a high level of elegance, with its letters adorned by a variety of additional strokes, as attested, for example, in fragments of the Genesis and Exodus scrolls from Wadi Murabbaᶜat

(figs. 52, 53), in a fragment of a Psalms scroll from Naḥal Ḥever (fig. 55), as well as in three Hebrew deeds dating from 134 CE, also from Naḥal Ḥever (fig. 65).

The "Jewish" cursive script fell into disuse shortly after the end of the Bar Kokhba revolt, a mute witness to the tragic fate that overcame the Jews in Judaea. The "Jewish" book-hand, however, continued to exist and developed into many different script styles, including various cursive styles among widely dispersed Jewish communities.

(*clockwise, from above*)

Fig. 61 *Epitaph of King Uzziah.*

Fig. 62. *"Loops" decorating letters on ossuaries.*

Fig. 64. *Cursive letters on ostraca from Masada.*

34

NH 46
◄ 16.2 cm ►

recto ◄

Fig. 63 (*above*). *Semi-cursive script in fragments of an Enoch scroll (4Q212).*

Fig. 65 (*left*). *A Hebrew deed from Naḥal Ḥever, 134* CE.

Ada Yardeni

Palaeography as a Tool for the Reading of Damaged Texts

Apart from the dating of undated written material, the acquaintance with the individual letter-signs often assists in *determining the readings* of damaged letters, or in the *deciphering of idiosyncratic handwritings*, a number of which is evidenced in the Qumran manuscripts. As an example let us take a *closer look* at a fragmentary text and try to confirm the reading of a few letters:

A fragment bearing the remains of a Halachic text labeled 4QMMT (*Miqtsat Ma*ᶜ*asei ha-Torah*) published by Elisha Qimron and John Strugnell in *DJD* 10, was written as a letter. This text is represented in several manuscripts, one of which (4Q397; fig. 66) was written in a formal script-style with personal features. We notice the irregularity of the script, reflecting a somewhat careless writing of a professional scribe. The letters differ in their heights and certain letters show slight variations in their appearance, but most of them can be easily identified.

The word *sha*ᶜ*atnez* (Shin, Ayin, Tet, Nun, Zayin) in line 7 of the second column (see figs. 66b,c) is very clear and so is the following *weshelo* (Waw, Shin, Lamed, Waw, Alef). The following word is somewhat damaged. The letter after Lamed cannot be Yod or Waw because these usually have a large "hook" at their top slanting down to the left. The only letter possible is Zayin, the top of which somewhat curves backwards (although not as much as that in the word *sha*ᶜ*atnez*). Of the last letter in this word only remains of its upper stroke have survived. The *small space* available for this letter, its *thickened top* and the *sharp slant of the stroke to the left*, as well as *a dot of ink* surviving of the left part of the damaged letter, leave no doubt as to its identification as Ayin, yielding the reading *lizroa* (Lamed, Zayin, Waw, Ayin).

Another example from the same column: the end of the second word in line 11 is damaged and only tops of the letters survive. The letter after the first He is a mere down-stroke. Given the fact that Waw and Yod have a "hook", we identify it as Zayin. This is followed by Waw or Yod. Then follow remains from the top of a

Fig. 66a. A detail of 4Q397 (photo: Israel Antiquities Authority).

Fig. 66b. *Remains of a column in 4Q397.*

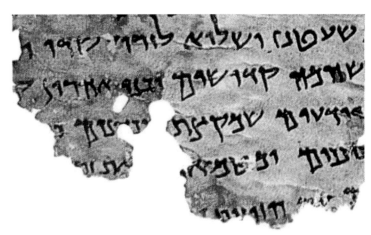

Fig. 66c. *Enlarged lines of the remains of a column in 4Q397.*

letter that bends backwards. This could again be Zayin but also Nun, *both having their tops bending backwards* (already indicating the early phases of the development of the group of seven letter-signs [Gimel, Zayin, Tet, Nun, Ayin, Tsadi and Shin] bearing similar flourishes in later Torah scrolls). There still remains the following letter with the "hook" (Waw or Yod) and the final letter, made of two elements, resembling the top of Taw. As for the same word appearing in line 4 (second word), we may read with certainty the word *hazonoth* (He, Zayin, Waw, Nun, Waw, Taw).

We have just seen how a *close acquaintance with the elements constructing the letter-signs* may help with the *reading* and the *restoration* of a damaged text.

We may now ask ourselves to which of the phases this fragment belongs. We may notice the *long, final Mem*, the *relative long Kaf, Pe and Tsadi*, the *curving backwards of the tops of Nun and Zayin*, and the *occasional bending at the right "arms" of Ayin and Shin*, while the right "arm" of Tsadi reflects a to-

and-fro movement. In view of these observations, the dating of this fragment seems to favor a *late Hasmonean* or *early Herodian* date, i.e., about the second half of the first century BCE. Most of the typical additional flourishes, especially in Nun and Zayin, *have not yet become independent strokes*, while the *double "roof" of He* is a Herodian rather than Hasmonean phenomenon.

A thorough palaeographical analysis is mostly used for the determination of stylistic features, common to several handwritings, whereas personal characteristics of a professional scribe are often distinct enough to reveal the handwriting of a particular scribe without requiring a profound palaeographical knowledge. So far, no classification of the different scribes in the Qumran corpus has been made. This may be a challenging project, which could add important information to the *scribal activity in Judaea in the Second Temple period*, also resolving the question of the *kind of compositions copied by each of the scribes* (see Yardeni 2007).

Early Characteristics in Pre-"Jewish" Manuscripts from Qumran

The earliest scrolls from Qumran date to the late third century BCE when their script still resembles the Aramaic script in its late stages. Thus, the script of 4QSam^b fragments (late third century BCE [fig. 37] is very close in form to the script of the Aramaic documents from Wadi ed-Daliyeh (SP=Samaria Papyri), the latest of which dates from 335 BCE (fig. 36). The script of SP1 is relatively narrow and more angular than that of earlier Aramaic documents and these features characterize also 4QSam^b. The distinction between medial and final forms of Kaf, Mem, Nun, and Pe already attested in SP1 is almost complete in 4QSam^b. However, the "leg" of Tsadi still has not curved its bottom to the left. No additional strokes appear in either document. In both documents, the medial forms of these letters are still extending below the imaginary base line, indicating that the medial forms developed from the final forms by curving their right down-strokes to the left and thus becoming shorter than the final forms. The final Mem, unlike the other final forms, developed from the medial Aramaic Mem, in that its left stroke became vertical, creating a rectangular form of the letter. In 4QSam^b the rectangle is already near closed whereas in SP1 the left stroke is still short, although the final Mem already differs from the medial Mem. Another early feature of 4QSam^b is the final form of Lamed, which resembles final forms of Lamed in third-century BCE Aramaic papyri (e.g., ostracon Aram. 4 from Edfu, Egypt; fig. 39), still not appearing in SP1, whereas the medial form already augurs its form in later Qumran scrolls. A short additional stroke, decending to the left from the top of the "mast" of Lamed, already appears in a third-century BCE Aramaic document from Egypt (LdV; fig. 38) and heralds the "hook" at the top of this letter evidenced in the later phases of the letter's development. In 4QSam^b, a final Yod also still appears, which is somewhat bigger than the medial form. In SP1 this difference is minor. The final Lamed and the final Yod disappear from the so-called "Jewish" script.

Although not from Qumran, but an important signpost in the transition from the Aramaic to the so-called "Jewish" script is the Nash Papyrus (fig. 27), the semi-cursive script of which resembles Aramaic documents from Egypt dating from about the late third century BCE, as well as the script of the Maresha ostracon from 176 BCE (fig. 26). However, certain letters, such as Bet, Tsadi and Taw, indicate a somewhat later date. It may perhaps be dated to around the mid-second century BCE. It is quite close to the later phase of evolution of the "Jewish" script appearing in the 1QIsa^a scroll from Qumran (fig. 46). Although not an elegant example of the "Jewish" script, it already contains certain additional strokes, such as the long "hook" of Lamed, the "hooks" of Waw and Yod, and the turning backwards of the top of Zayin. The final Nun is still wavy like in the Aramaic script but some of the medial forms, as well as some of the Gimels, already have a thick top. These are the early representatives of the flourishes to the group of the seven letters decorated in later Torah scrolls.

Author's Hints

**Some typical features of the Early- and Mid-Hasmonean Formal Script
(second to early first centuries BCE):**

- Mostly no "tail" at the lower right corner of Bet.
- "Hooks" at the tops of Waw, Yod, and Lamed.
- A long final Mem occasionally open at its left lower corner.
- Open Samekh at its left lower corner.
- Mostly a small, short Ayin.
- Medial Kaf, Mem, Pe, Tsadi extending below the imaginary base line.
- Tet with a short, slanting base-stroke.
- Qof with a short "leg".

When most of these features appear together the manuscript probably belongs to the **Hasmonean period.**

**Some typical features of the Late Hasmonean or Early Herodian Formal Script
(mid-first century BCE to early first century CE):**

- The beginning of the leveling of letter heights
- The sporadic appearance of additional short strokes at the left leg of Alef, and at the top of Gimel, Zayin and Nun.
- Angular joints between the right vertical down-stroke and the base stroke
- The base stroke of Bet mostly extending beyond its meeting point with the right down-stroke, creating a "tail" at the right lower corner of the letter.
- Closed Samekh and final Mem.
- He with a fat or triangular addition at the left end of its "roof".

When most of these features appear together the manuscript probably belongs to the **Late Hasmonean or Early Herodian period.**

**Some typical features of the Late Herodian Formal Script
(early first century to 70 CE):**

- The top of the right "arm" of Alef and Tsadi and the middle "arm" of Shin made with a to-and-fro movement.
- The bottom of the left down-stroke of Alef and the "nose" of Pe bending backwards to the right.
- Horizontal base-strokes of Bet, Tet and Kaf.
- Bet and Kaf sometimes identical in their form.
- An additional short stroke appearing sporadically at the top of the left down-stroke of Tet, Ayin, Tsadi and Shin.
- Ayin with a long right stroke, bending or curving and slanting down to the left and reaching the imaginary base line.
- A short, final Mem, its left down-stroke occasionally not touching the "roof".

When most of these features appear together the manuscript probably belongs to the **Late Herodian period.**

Select Bibliography

Avigad, N.
1958   "The Palaeography of the Dead Sea Scrolls and Related Documents," *Scripta Hierosolymitana*, Publications of the Hebrew University, IV (Jerusalem), pp. 56–87.

Cohen, Y.
2014 (תשע"ד)   יכתיבה, קריאה ואוריינות במזרח הקדום', קתדרה 251, עמ' 167-182.

Cross, F. M., Jr.
1961a   "The Development of the Jewish Scripts," *The Bible and the Ancient Near East*, Essays in Honor of W. F. Albright (ed. G. E. Wright; Garden City), pp. 133–202.
1961b   *The Ancient Library of Qumran 2*. Garden City.
1962   "The Palaeographical Dating of the Copper Document," in: M. Baillet, J. T. Milik and R. de Vaux, *DJD* III (Oxford), pp. 217–221.

Doudna, G. L.
forthcoming   The Sect of the Qumran Texts and Its Leading Role in the Temple in Jerusalem During Much of the First Century BCE: Toward a New Framework for Understanding.

Haran, M.
1981 (תשמ"א)   'מלאכת הסופר בתקופת המקרא - מגילות הספרים ואביזרי הכתיבה', תרביץ נ, עמ' 65-87.
1988   "On the Diffusion of Literacy and Schools in Ancient Israel," *Vetus Testamentum* Supplement, pp. 81–95.

Jull, A. J., D. J. Donahue, M. Broshi, and E. Tov
1995   "Radiocarbon Dating of Scrolls and Linen Fragments from the Judean Desert," *Radiocarbon* 37, pp. 11–19.

Naveh, J.
1970   *The Development of the Aramaic Script*, The Israel Academy of Sciences and Humanities, Proceedings V/1. Jerusalem.
1982   *Early History of the Alphabet*. Jerusalem.
2009   *Studies in West-Semitic Epigraphy*. Jerusalem.

Porten, B. and A. Yardeni
1986–1999   *Textbook of Aramaic Documents from Ancient Egypt*, vols. 1–4. Jerusalem.

Qimron, E. and J. Strugnell
1994   "Qumran Cave 4: V. Miqsat Maᶜase ha-Torah," *DJD* 10 (Oxford), Pls. IV, V–VI.

Rainey, A. F.
1969 (תשכ"ט)   'הסופר באוגרית מעמדו והשפעתו', דברי האקדמיה הלאומית הישראלית למדעים, כרך רביעי. חוברת 2, ירושלים.

Tov, E. (ed.)
1993   *The Dead Sea Scrolls on Microfiche: A Comprehensive Facsimile Edition of the Texts from the Judaean Desert*. Printed Catalog by S. Reed, Israel Antiquity Authority. Leiden.

Tov, E.
2000   "Further Evidence for the Existence of a Qumran School," *The Dead Sea Scrolls, Fifty Years after Their Discovery 1947–1997* (Jerusalem), pp. 199–216.

Yardeni, A.
1991a   "Remarks on the Priestly Blessing on Two Amulets from Jerusalem," *Vetus Testamentum* 41, pp. 176–185.
1991b   "The Palaeography of 4QJerᵃ: A Comparative Study," *Textus* 15, pp. 233–268.
1994   "Script," in: E. Qimron and J. Strugnell, *DJD* 10 (Oxford), 21–25.
1996   "Palaeography," in: J. Baumgarten, The Damascus Document (4Q266–273), *DJD* 18 (Oxford), p. 124.
1997   *The Book of Hebrew Script* (Jerusalem; The British Library edition 2002).
2000   *Textbook of Aramaic, Hebrew and Nabataean Documentary Texts from the Judaean Desert and Related Material* (Jerusalem), vols. A and B.
2007   "A Note on a Qumran Scribe," in: M. Lubetski (ed.), *New Seals and Inscriptions, Hebrew, Idumean, and Cuneiform* (Sheffield Phoenix Press), pp. 287–298.